처음 시작하는 초등 영문법

완전 정복 초등 영문법

Workbook

3

1	**answer**	답하다	Jenny can **answer** the question. 제니는 그 질문에 대답할 수 있다.
2	**at night**	밤에	You must not watch TV **at night**. 너는 밤에 TV를 보면 안 된다.
3	**bring**	가져오다	Tom doesn't have to **bring** his lunch. 톰은 그의 점심을 가져올 필요가 없다.
4	**brush**	닦다	You had better **brush** your teeth. 너는 이를 닦는 것이 좋겠다.
5	**carefully**	주의 깊게	She has to listen **carefully**. 그녀는 주의 깊게 들어야 한다.
6	**climb**	오르다	He should not **climb** a mountain. 그는 등산을 하지 않는 것이 좋겠다.
7	**enter**	들어가다	He doesn't **enter** this room. 그는 이 방에 들어가지 않는다.
8	**every day**	매일	She has to exercise **every day**. 그녀는 매일 운동해야 한다.
9	**exercise**	운동하다	They always **exercise** after work. 그들은 일을 마친 후 항상 운동한다.
10	**fruit**	과일	I had better eat more **fruit**. 나는 과일을 더 먹는 것이 좋겠다.
11	**get up**	일어나다	She is able to **get up** early. 그녀는 일찍 일어날 수 있다.
12	**go out**	외출하다	She should not **go out**. 그녀는 외출하지 않는 것이 좋겠다.
13	**had better**	~하는 것이 좋겠다	You **had better** leave now. 너는 지금 떠나는 것이 좋겠다.
14	**hurry**	서두르다	He should not **hurry**. 그는 서두르지 않는 것이 좋겠다.
15	**invite**	초대하다	We are able to **invite** him. 우리는 그를 초대할 수 있다.

16	**leave**	떠나다	You'd better **leave** for Seoul now. 너는 지금 서울로 떠나는 것이 좋겠다.
17	**museum**	박물관	I have to go to the **museum**. 나는 박물관에 가야 한다.
18	**must**	해야 한다	I **must** study math. 나는 수학을 공부해야 한다.
19	**pass**	통과하다	I cannot **pass** the test. 나는 그 시험을 통과할 수 없다.
20	**problem**	문제	You can solve the **problem**. 너는 그 문제를 풀 수 있다.
21	**question**	질문	Jenny can answer this **question**. 제니는 이 질문에 대답할 수 있다.
22	**quiet**	조용한	We should be **quiet**. 우리는 조용히 하는 것이 좋겠다.
23	**rest**	휴식	He has to take a **rest**. 그는 휴식해야 한다.
24	**solve**	풀다	The boy can **solve** the problem. 그 소년은 그 문제를 풀 수 있다.
25	**stay**	머무르다	He may **stay** here. 그는 이곳에 머물지도 모른다.
26	**try**	노력하다	The boys must **try** hard. 그 소년들은 열심히 노력해야 한다.
27	**use**	사용하다	Is your dad able to **use** a computer? 너의 아빠는 컴퓨터를 사용할 수 있니?
28	**vegetable**	야채	He eats **vegetables** every morning. 그는 매일 아침 야채를 먹는다.
29	**wait**	기다리다	Students have to **wait** in the classroom. 학생들은 교실에서 기다려야 한다.
30	**worry**	걱정하다	You don't have to **worry**. 너는 걱정할 필요가 없다.

A 다음 우리말 뜻에 해당하는 영어 단어를 쓰세요.

❶ 해야 한다 ⟶ ______

❷ 주의 깊게 ⟶ ______

❸ 들어가다 ⟶ ______

❹ 휴식 ⟶ ______

❺ 떠나다 ⟶ ______

❻ 답하다 ⟶ ______

❼ 질문 ⟶ ______

❽ 노력하다 ⟶ ______

❾ 운동하다 ⟶ ______

❿ 외출하다 ⟶ ______

⓫ 오르다 ⟶ ______

⓬ 과일 ⟶ ______

⓭ 사용하다 ⟶ ______

⓮ 기다리다 ⟶ ______

⓯ 조용한 ⟶ ______

B 다음 영어 단어에 해당하는 우리말 뜻을 쓰세요.

1. solve → ______
2. invite → ______
3. problem → ______
4. get up → ______
5. stay → ______
6. hurry → ______
7. pass → ______
8. museum → ______
9. worry → ______
10. bring → ______
11. had better → ______
12. vegetable → ______
13. every day → ______
14. at night → ______
15. brush → ______

A 영어는 우리말로, 우리말은 영어로 쓰세요.

1. can ____________
2. may ____________
3. must ____________
4. sing ____________
5. leave ____________
6. stop ____________
7. cook ____________
8. vegetable ____________
9. early ____________
10. tennis ____________
11. 배고픈 ____________
12. 바이올린 ____________
13. 풀다 ____________
14. 문제 ____________
15. 일어나다 ____________
16. 머무르다 ____________
17. 통과하다 ____________
18. 고치다 ____________
19. (그림을) 그리다 ____________
20. 싫어하다 ____________

B 괄호 안에서 알맞은 것을 고르세요.

1. He can (dance / dances) well.
2. She must (gets / get) up early.
3. Tom may (cooks / cook) pizza.
4. We can (watches / watch) TV.
5. You (can solve / solve can) the problem.
6. She (may be / be may) late for school.
7. I (must pass / pass must) the test.
8. You (eat must / must eat) vegetables.
9. I (may go / go may) to the park.
10. My sister (can paint / paint can) well.

C 괄호 안에 주어진 단어를 이용해서 빈칸을 완성하세요.

1. He ____________________ well. (can / dance)
2. She ____________________ early. (get up / must)
3. Tom ____________________ pizza. (cook / may)
4. We ____________________ TV. (watch / can)
5. You ____________________ the problem. (can / solve)
6. She ____________________ late for school. (be / may)
7. I ____________________ the test. (pass / must)
8. You ____________________ vegetables. (eat / must)
9. I ____________________ to the park. (may / go)
10. My sister ____________________ well. (paint / can)

D 우리말과 같도록 괄호 안의 말을 이용해서 문장을 완성하세요.

1. 그는 춤을 잘 출 수 있다. (can / dance / He / well)

   ____ .

2. 너는 그 문제를 풀 수 있다. (You / solve / the problem / can)

   ____ .

3. 나는 그 시험을 통과해야 한다. (pass / I / must / the test)

   ____ .

4. 그녀는 학교에 늦을지도 모른다. (late for school / be / may / She)

   ____ .

5. 톰은 피자를 요리할지도 모른다. (Tom / pizza / may / cook)

   ____ .

A 영어는 우리말로, 우리말은 영어로 쓰세요.

❶ bicycle ______________

❷ speak ______________

❸ go home ______________

❹ guitar ______________

❺ walk ______________

❻ answer ______________

❼ question ______________

❽ breakfast ______________

❾ scissors ______________

❿ dinner ______________

⓫ 운전하다 ______________

⓬ 사용하다 ______________

⓭ 영화 ______________

⓮ 초대하다 ______________

⓯ 파티 ______________

⓰ 숙제 ______________

⓱ 도와주다 ______________

⓲ 열다 ______________

⓳ 야구 ______________

⓴ 사진, 그림 ______________

B 괄호 안에서 알맞은 것을 고르세요.

❶ He (can / is able) speak English.

❷ I (am able / can) to sing the song.

❸ The baby (can / is able) to walk.

❹ He (cannot / is not) able to play soccer.

❺ They (are not / cannot) able to go home.

❻ Mr. Brown (is not / cannot) fix the computer.

❼ (Is the dog / Can the dog) able to run fast?

❽ (Are you / Can you) get up early?

❾ (Can you / Are you) answer the question?

❿ (Are they / Can they) do their homework?

C 괄호 안에 주어진 단어를 이용해서 빈칸을 완성하세요.

1. He ____________________ English. (can / speak)
2. I ____________________ the song. (am able to / sing)
3. The baby ____________________. (walk / is able to)
4. He ____________________ soccer. (is not able to / play)
5. They ____________________ home. (go / are not able to)
6. Mr. Brown ____________________ the computer. (fix / cannot)
7. _________ the dog ______________ fast? (Is / able to run)
8. _________ you ______________ early? (get up / Can)
9. _________ you ______________ the question? (Can / answer)
10. _________ they ______________ their homework? (do / Can)

D 우리말과 같도록 괄호 안의 말을 이용해서 문장을 완성하세요.

1. 그는 영어를 말할 수 있다. (can / speak / English / He)

   ____ .

2. 나는 그 노래를 부를 수 있다. (the song / sing / am able to / I)

   ____ .

3. 그는 축구를 할 수 없다. (He / is not / play soccer / able to)

   ____ .

4. 너는 일찍 일어날 수 있니? (Can / early / get up / you)

   ____ ?

5. 그 개는 빨리 달릴 수 있니? (Is / able to / the dog / run fast)

   ____ ?

A 영어는 우리말로, 우리말은 영어로 쓰세요.

❶ must	________	⓫ 매일	________
❷ clean	________	⓬ 기다리다	________
❸ listen	________	⓭ 수학	________
❹ carefully	________	⓮ 만나다	________
❺ eat	________	⓯ 농구	________
❻ food	________	⓰ 테니스	________
❼ try	________	⓱ 밤에	________
❽ exercise	________	⓲ 박물관	________
❾ late	________	⓳ 걱정하다	________
❿ library	________	⓴ 가져오다	________

B 괄호 안에서 알맞은 것을 고르세요.

❶ You (must / have) clean your room.

❷ I (must / have) to help my mom.

❸ He (must / has) to go to the park.

❹ We (must / have) get up early.

❺ They (not must / don't have to) study math.

❻ They (don't have / must not) drink water.

❼ We (must not / don't have) run in the museum.

❽ She (not must / doesn't have to) bring her lunch.

❾ You (don’t have to / not must) clean your room.

❿ Dan (must not / don't have) come home late.

C 괄호 안에 주어진 단어를 이용해서 빈칸을 완성하세요.

1. You ________________ your room. (must / clean)
2. I ________________ my mom. (help / have to)
3. He ________________ to the park. (has to / go)
4. We ________________ early. (must / get up)
5. They ________________ math. (don't have to / study)
6. They ________________ water. (drink / must not)
7. We ________________ in the museum. (run / must not)
8. She ________________ her lunch. (doesn't have to / bring)
9. You ________________ your room. (don't have to / clean)
10. Dan ________________ home late. (come / must not)

D 우리말과 같도록 괄호 안의 말을 이용해서 문장을 완성하세요.

1. 나는 나의 엄마를 도와야 한다. (have to / help / my mom / I)

   ________________________________.

2. 그는 공원에 가야 한다. (to the park / go / has to / He)

   ________________________________.

3. 그들은 물을 마시면 안 된다. (They / must / drink / not / water)

   ________________________________.

4. 그녀는 그녀의 점심을 가져올 필요가 없다. (doesn't have to / She / bring / her lunch)

   ________________________________.

5. 우리는 일찍 일어나야 한다. (early / We / get up / must)

   ________________________________.

A 영어는 우리말로, 우리말은 영어로 쓰세요.

1. had better ____________
2. wear ____________
3. enter ____________
4. rest ____________
5. sleep ____________
6. coat ____________
7. there ____________
8. go out ____________
9. here ____________
10. mountain ____________
11. 오르다 ____________
12. 과일 ____________
13. 조용한 ____________
14. 저녁, 저녁 식사 ____________
15. 지도 ____________
16. 가져오다 ____________
17. 서두르다 ____________
18. 할머니 ____________
19. 부엌 ____________
20. 솔질하다 ____________

B 괄호 안에서 알맞은 것을 고르세요.

1. I (should / had) eat vegetables.
2. You (should / had) better wear a coat.
3. My brother (should / had) study hard.
4. (You'd / You'had) better leave for Seoul.
5. (He'had / He'd) better meet her.
6. He should not (enters / enter) this room.
7. We should (are / be) quiet in the library.
8. We'd better not (goes / go) to the park.
9. I'd better (not stay / stay not) home.
10. He (should not / not should) climb a mountain.

C 괄호 안에 주어진 단어를 이용해서 빈칸을 완성하세요.

1. I ______________ vegetables. (eat / should)
2. You ______________ a coat. (wear / had better)
3. My brother ______________ hard. (should / study)
4. ______________ for Seoul. (You'd better / leave)
5. ______________ her. (meet / He'd better)
6. He ______________ this room. (should not / enter)
7. We ______________ quiet in the library. (should / be)
8. ______________ to the park. (We'd better not / go)
9. ______________ home. (stay / I'd better not)
10. He ______________ a mountain. (should not / climb)

D 우리말과 같도록 괄호 안의 말을 이용해서 문장을 완성하세요.

1. 나는 채소를 먹는 것이 좋겠다. (should / vegetables / eat / I)

   ______________________________ .

2. 너는 코트를 입는 것이 좋겠다. (a coat / wear / You / had better)

   ______________________________ .

3. 그는 등산을 하지 않는 것이 좋겠다. (He / climb a mountain / should / not)

   ______________________________ .

4. 우리는 공원에 가지 않는 것이 좋겠다. (go / to the park / not / We'd better)

   ______________________________ .

5. 나는 집에 머무르지 않는 것이 좋겠다. (stay home / I'd better / not)

   ______________________________ .

1	**around**	주위에	The earth moves **around** the sun. 지구는 태양 주위를 돈다.
2	**bank**	은행	They work at a **bank**. 그들은 은행에서 일한다.
3	**beautiful**	아름다운	She isn't **beautiful**. 그녀는 아름답지 않다.
4	**call**	전화하다	He **calls** you every night. 그는 매일 밤 너에게 전화한다.
5	**catch**	잡다	Andy doesn't **catch** the ball. 앤디는 그 공을 잡지 않는다.
6	**church**	교회	They go to **church** every Sunday. 그들은 일요일마다 교회에 간다.
7	**class**	반, 학급	Sally and I are in the same **class**. 샐리와 나는 같은 반이다.
8	**earth**	지구	The **earth** is round. 지구는 둥글다.
9	**east**	동쪽	The sun rises in the **east**. 태양은 동쪽에서 뜬다.
10	**every Monday**	월요일마다	Does he study English **every Monday**? 그는 월요일마다 영어를 공부하니?
11	**every morning**	매일 아침	Do you have breakfast **every morning**? 너는 매일 아침 식사를 하니?
12	**expensive**	비싼	These aren't **expensive**. 이것들은 비싸지 않다.
13	**flower**	꽃	Does your mother like **flowers**? 너의 엄마는 꽃을 좋아하니?
14	**hospital**	병원	Sue and Tom work at the **hospital**. 수와 톰은 병원에서 일한다.
15	**kitchen**	부엌	My mom isn't in the **kitchen**. 나의 엄마는 부엌에 있지 않다.

No.	Word	Meaning	Example
16	**live**	살다	They don't **live** in Seoul. 그들은 서울에 살지 않는다.
17	**move**	움직이다	Luka can't **move** his body. 루카는 그의 몸을 움직일 수 없다.
18	**parent**	부모	He visits his **parents** during the holiday. 그는 휴일 동안 부모님을 방문한다.
19	**rise**	(해, 달이) 뜨다	Does the sun **rise** in the east? 해는 동쪽에서 뜨니?
20	**round**	둥근	I have a **round** table. 나는 둥근 식탁이 있다.
21	**same**	같은	The animals use the **same** place. 동물들은 같은 장소를 이용한다.
22	**science**	과학	Jamie likes **science**. 제이미는 과학을 좋아한다.
23	**set**	(해, 달이) 지다	The sun **sets** in the west. 해는 서쪽으로 진다.
24	**spider**	거미	**Spiders** have eight legs. 거미는 여덟 개의 다리를 가지고 있다.
25	**strong**	강한, 힘 센	Is the superman **strong**? 그 슈퍼맨은 힘이 세니?
26	**together**	함께	We often play **together**. 우리는 종종 함께 논다.
27	**wall**	벽	**Walls** have ears. 벽에도 귀가 있다.
28	**wash**	씻다	She **washes** her hair every day. 그녀는 매일 머리를 감는다.
29	**west**	서쪽	Stars set in the **west**. 별들은 서쪽으로 진다.
30	**worm**	벌레	Birds eat lots of **worms**. 새는 많은 벌레를 먹는다.

A 다음 우리말 뜻에 해당하는 영어 단어를 쓰세요.

❶ (해, 달이) 뜨다 ⟶ ______________________

❷ (해, 달이) 지다 ⟶ ______________________

❸ 반, 학급 ⟶ ______________________

❹ 같은 ⟶ ______________________

❺ 살다 ⟶ ______________________

❻ 은행 ⟶ ______________________

❼ 병원 ⟶ ______________________

❽ 지구 ⟶ ______________________

❾ 부엌 ⟶ ______________________

❿ 둥근 ⟶ ______________________

⓫ 부모 ⟶ ______________________

⓬ 벽 ⟶ ______________________

⓭ 잡다 ⟶ ______________________

⓮ 비싼 ⟶ ______________________

⓯ 벌레 ⟶ ______________________

B 다음 영어 단어에 해당하는 우리말 뜻을 쓰세요.

1. east → ________
2. around → ________
3. flower → ________
4. west → ________
5. science → ________
6. church → ________
7. move → ________
8. call → ________
9. strong → ________
10. together → ________
11. wash → ________
12. beautiful → ________
13. every morning → ________
14. every Monday → ________
15. spider → ________

A 영어는 우리말로, 우리말은 영어로 쓰세요.

① live	________	⑪ 주위에	________
② hospital	________	⑫ 서쪽	________
③ earth	________	⑬ (해, 달이) 지다	________
④ round	________	⑭ 과학	________
⑤ rise	________	⑮ 움직이다	________
⑥ wall	________	⑯ 할아버지	________
⑦ catch	________	⑰ 박물관	________
⑧ worm	________	⑱ 함께	________
⑨ east	________	⑲ 씻다	________
⑩ every morning	________	⑳ 거미	________

B 괄호 안에서 알맞은 것을 고르세요.

① I (working / work) at the hospital.

② Walls (having / have) ears.

③ He (is / being) a doctor.

④ Three plus two (being / is) five.

⑤ They (going / go) to the library every day.

⑥ The earth (being / is) round.

⑦ We often (play / playing) together.

⑧ They (living / live) in London.

⑨ The early bird (catches / catching) the worm.

⑩ Ants (having / have) six legs.

C 괄호 안에 주어진 단어를 이용해서 빈칸을 완성하세요.

1. ______________________ at the hospital. (I / work)
2. ______________________ ears. (have / Walls)
3. ______________________ a doctor. (He / is)
4. ______________________ five. (is / Three plus two)
5. ______________________ to the library every day. (go / They)
6. ______________________ round. (The earth / is)
7. ______________________ together. (often play / We)
8. ______________________ in London. (They / live)
9. ______________________ the worm. (The early bird / catches)
10. ______________________ six legs. (have / Ants)

D 우리말과 같도록 괄호 안의 말을 이용해서 문장을 완성하세요.

1. 나는 병원에서 일한다. (work / at the hospital / I)

   ______________________________________ .

2. 지구는 둥글다. (is / round / The earth)

   ______________________________________ .

3. 그는 의사다. (is / He / a doctor)

   ______________________________________ .

4. 그들은 런던에 산다. (They / in London / live)

   ______________________________________ .

5. 벽에도 귀가 있다. (have / ears / Walls)

   ______________________________________ .

A 영어는 우리말로, 우리말은 영어로 쓰세요.

1. hungry ____________
2. bank ____________
3. cook ____________
4. kitchen ____________
5. parent ____________
6. catch ____________
7. happy ____________
8. expensive ____________
9. orange ____________
10. pretty ____________
11. 매일 ____________
12. 꽃 ____________
13. 월요일마다 ____________
14. 축구 ____________
15. 교회 ____________
16. 전화하다 ____________
17. 강한, 힘 센 ____________
18. 반, 학급 ____________
19. 같은 ____________
20. 아름다운 ____________

B 괄호 안에서 알맞은 것을 고르세요.

1. You (isn't / aren't) late.
2. I (am not / isn't) happy.
3. We (don't / doesn't) eat breakfast.
4. He (don't / doesn't) like oranges.
5. (Is / Are) Ellie your friend?
6. (Are / Am) we late?
7. (Am / Is) he strong?
8. (Do / Does) he study English every Monday?
9. (Do / Does) the sun rise in the east?
10. (Do / Does) they go to church every Sunday?

C 괄호 안에 주어진 단어를 이용해서 빈칸을 완성하세요.

❶ ____________________ late. (You / aren't)

❷ ____________________ happy. (am not / I)

❸ ____________________ breakfast. (don't eat / We)

❹ ____________________ oranges. (doesn't like / He)

❺ ____________________ your friend? (Ellie / Is)

❻ ____________________ late? (we / Are)

❼ ____________________ strong? (he / Is)

❽ ____________________ English every Monday? (study / Does he)

❾ ____________________ in the east? (Does the sun / rise)

❿ ____________________ to church every Sunday? (go / Do they)

D 우리말과 같도록 괄호 안의 말을 이용해서 문장을 완성하세요.

❶ 우리는 아침을 먹지 않는다. (don't / breakfast / We / eat)

____ .

❷ 나는 행복하지 않다. (I / not / am / happy)

____ .

❸ 그는 힘이 세니? (he / Is / strong)

____ ?

❹ 해는 동쪽에서 뜨니? (rise / the sun / Does / in the east)

____ ?

❺ 그들은 일요일마다 교회에 가니? (Do / every Sunday / they / go to church)

____ ?

1	**across**	가로질러	She is walking **across** the street. 그녀는 길을 가로질러 걷고 있다.
2	**airplane**	비행기	They make a paper **airplane**. 그들은 종이 비행기를 만든다.
3	**art museum**	미술관	We are going to the **art museum**. 우리는 미술관에 가고 있다.
4	**bathroom**	욕실	Mom cleans the **bathroom**. 엄마는 욕실을 청소한다.
5	**believe**	믿다	I don't **believe** the news. 나는 그 뉴스를 믿지 않는다.
6	**cross**	건너다	Are they **crossing** the street? 그들은 길을 건너고 있니?
7	**dentist**	치과의사	I have to go to the **dentist**. 나는 치과에 가야 한다.
8	**diary**	일기	You are writing a **diary**. 너는 일기를 쓰고 있다.
9	**die**	죽다	The fish are **dying**. 물고기들이 죽어가고 있다.
10	**family**	가족	He loves his **family**. 그는 그의 가족을 사랑한다.
11	**forget**	잊다	They **forget** about me. 그들은 나에 대해 잊는다.
12	**grass**	잔디	We are sitting on the **grass**. 우리는 잔디에 앉아 있다.
13	**hear**	듣다	What can you **hear**? 너는 무엇이 들리니?
14	**history**	역사	I am not studying **history**. 나는 역사를 공부하고 있지 않다.
15	**lie**	눕다	Is your cat **lying** on the sofa? 너의 고양이는 소파에 누워 있니?

16	**loudly**	크게	They are speaking **loudly**. 그들은 크게 말하고 있다.
17	**music**	음악	He is listening to **music**. 그는 음악을 듣고 있다.
18	**push**	밀다	The boy **pushes** me. 그 소년은 나를 민다.
19	**smell**	냄새나다	The bread **smells** good. 그 빵은 냄새가 좋다.
20	**street**	거리	She walks down the **street**. 그녀는 거리를 걸어 내려간다.
21	**swim**	수영하다	They are **swimming** in a pool. 그들은 수영장에서 수영하고 있다.
22	**take pictures**	사진 찍다	Dad is **taking pictures** now. 아빠는 지금 사진을 찍고 있다.
23	**telephone**	전화기	Is he using a **telephone**? 그는 전화기를 사용하고 있니?
24	**track**	트랙	She is running on a **track**. 그녀는 트랙 위를 달리고 있다.
25	**trip**	여행	We are planning a **trip**. 우리는 여행을 계획하고 있다.
26	**umbrella**	우산	I have an **umbrella**. 나는 우산을 가지고 있다.
27	**visit**	방문하다	She is going to **visit** London. 그녀는 런던을 방문할 것이다.
28	**war**	전쟁	A lot of people are dying in the **war**. 많은 사람들이 그 전쟁에서 죽어가고 있다.
29	**wish**	소망하다	I **wish** to go there. 나는 거기에 가고 싶다.
30	**write**	쓰다	Mom is **writing** a letter now. 엄마는 지금 편지를 쓰고 있다.

A 다음 우리말 뜻에 해당하는 영어 단어를 쓰세요.

❶ 냄새나다 → ______

❷ 가로질러 → ______

❸ 눕다 → ______

❹ 비행기 → ______

❺ 건너다 → ______

❻ 죽다 → ______

❼ 거리 → ______

❽ 듣다 → ______

❾ 트랙 → ______

❿ 믿다 → ______

⓫ 방문하다 → ______

⓬ 잊다 → ______

⓭ 역사 → ______

⓮ 치과의사 → ______

⓯ 우산 → ______

/30

B 다음 영어 단어에 해당하는 우리말 뜻을 쓰세요.

❶ loudly → ______

❷ wish → ______

❸ swim → ______

❹ write → ______

❺ grass → ______

❻ diary → ______

❼ bathroom → ______

❽ trip → ______

❾ push → ______

❿ family → ______

⓫ music → ______

⓬ take pictures → ______

⓭ art museum → ______

⓮ telephone → ______

⓯ war → ______

A 영어는 우리말로, 우리말은 영어로 쓰세요.

❶ cook	______	⓫ 쓰다	______
❷ need	______	⓬ 오르다	______
❸ hate	______	⓭ 함께	______
❹ smell	______	⓮ 거리	______
❺ hear	______	⓯ 걷다	______
❻ believe	______	⓰ 산	______
❼ forget	______	⓱ 들어가다	______
❽ umbrella	______	⓲ 밀다	______
❾ face	______	⓳ 햄버거	______
❿ homework	______	⓴ 가족	______

B 괄호 안에서 알맞은 것을 고르세요.

❶ I (am cooking / am cook) dinner.

❷ She (is drive / is driving) a car.

❸ I (am having / have) an umbrella.

❹ He (is loving / loves) his family.

❺ They (are watching / are watch) TV now.

❻ You (are having / are have) lunch.

❼ They (know / are knowing) me.

❽ Mom (is writing / is write) a letter.

❾ I (am clean / am cleaning) my room now.

❿ It (is smelling / smells) good.

C 괄호 안에 주어진 단어를 이용해서 빈칸을 완성하세요.

1. ______________ dinner. (am cooking / I)
2. ______________ a car. (She / is driving)
3. ______________ an umbrella. (have / I)
4. ______________ his family. (He / loves)
5. ______________ TV now. (are watching / They)
6. ______________ lunch. (You / are having)
7. ______________ me. (know / They)
8. ______________ a letter. (is writing / Mom)
9. ______________ my room now. (I / am cleaning)
10. ______________ good. (smells / It)

D 우리말과 같도록 괄호 안의 말을 이용해서 문장을 완성하세요.

1. 그녀는 자동차를 운전하고 있다. (is / driving / a car / She)

   ______________________________ .

2. 그는 그의 가족을 사랑한다. (He / his family / loves)

   ______________________________ .

3. 너는 저녁 식사를 하고 있다. (having / are / You / dinner)

   ______________________________ .

4. 나는 지금 나의 방을 청소하고 있다. (I / my room / am / cleaning / now)

   ______________________________ .

5. 그들은 나를 안다. (me / They / know)

   ______________________________ .

A 영어는 우리말로, 우리말은 영어로 쓰세요.

❶ river	________	⓫ 돕다	________
❷ lie	________	⓬ 앉다	________
❸ die	________	⓭ 기다리다	________
❹ stop	________	⓮ 일기	________
❺ track	________	⓯ 벤치	________
❻ letter	________	⓰ 바닥, 층	________
❼ museum	________	⓱ 풍선	________
❽ dentist	________	⓲ 신문	________
❾ speak	________	⓳ 도로, 길	________
❿ dance	________	⓴ 전쟁	________

B 괄호 안에서 알맞은 것을 고르세요.

❶ He (is eat / is eating) lunch now.

❷ All flowers (are dying / are die).

❸ He is (running / run) on the road.

❹ The man is (stop / stopping) a car.

❺ The man (is give / is giving) a balloon to a girl.

❻ We (are sing / are singing) now.

❼ Children (are swimming / are swim) now.

❽ The boy is (lie / lying) on the sofa.

❾ We are (sit / sitting) on the grass.

❿ He (is going / is go) to the library now.

C 괄호 안에 주어진 단어를 이용해서 빈칸을 완성하세요.

1. He ______________________ lunch now. (is / eating)
2. All flowers ______________________. (dying / are)
3. He ______________________ on the road. (running / is)
4. The man ______________________ a car. (is / stopping)
5. The man ______________________ a balloon to a girl. (giving / is)
6. We ______________________ now. (are / singing)
7. Children ______________________ now. (swimming / are)
8. The boy ______________________ on the sofa. (lying / is)
9. We ______________________ on the grass. (are / sitting)
10. He ______________________ to the library now. (going / is)

D 우리말과 같도록 괄호 안의 말을 이용해서 문장을 완성하세요.

1. 그는 지금 점심을 먹고 있다. (eating / is / lunch / He / now)

   ____ .

2. 그 남자가 자동차를 세우고 있다. (The man / is / a car / stopping)

   ____ .

3. 그 소년은 소파 위에 누워 있다. (lying / The boy / on the sofa / is)

   ____ .

4. 우리는 잔디에 앉아 있다. (We / on the grass / are / sitting)

   ____ .

5. 그 남자가 한 소녀에게 풍선을 주고 있다. (a balloon / giving / is / The man / to a girl)

   ____ .

A 영어는 우리말로, 우리말은 영어로 쓰세요.

1. take pictures ____________
2. walk ____________
3. trip ____________
4. homework ____________
5. clean ____________
6. visit ____________
7. history ____________
8. across ____________
9. loudly ____________
10. plan ____________
11. 아침, 아침 식사 ____________
12. 기타 ____________
13. 잔디 ____________
14. 벽 ____________
15. 그리다, 칠하다 ____________
16. 욕실 ____________
17. 여행 ____________
18. 과학 ____________
19. 영화 ____________
20. 길, 거리 ____________

B 괄호 안에서 알맞은 것을 고르세요.

1. I am (not baking / baking not) cookies.
2. She (isn't taking / taking isn't) a bath.
3. You (aren't playing / playing aren't) the guitar.
4. The boy is (not cleaning / cleaning not) the bathroom.
5. We are (planning not / not planning) a trip.
6. They are (not lying / lying not) on the grass.
7. I am (using not / not using) a computer.
8. Paul is (taking not / not taking) pictures.
9. The flower (dying isn't / isn't dying).
10. Dad (is not cooking / not is cooking) dinner.

C 괄호 안에 주어진 단어를 이용해서 빈칸을 완성하세요.

1. I ______________ cookies. (am not / baking)
2. She ______________ a bath. (isn't / taking)
3. You ______________ the guitar. (playing / aren't)
4. The boy ______________ the bathroom. (is not / cleaning)
5. We ______________ a trip. (planning / are not)
6. They ______________ on the grass. (are not / lying)
7. I ______________ a computer. (using / am not)
8. Paul ______________ pictures. (is not / taking)
9. The flower ______________. (dying / isn't)
10. Dad ______________ dinner. (cooking / is not)

D 우리말과 같도록 괄호 안의 말을 이용해서 문장을 완성하세요.

1. 나는 쿠키를 굽고 있지 않다. (am not / baking / I / cookies)

   ______________________________ .

2. 너는 기타를 치고 있지 않다. (You / the guitar / playing / aren't)

   ______________________________ .

3. 그 꽃은 죽어가고 있지 않다. (isn't / The flower / dying)

   ______________________________ .

4. 우리는 여행을 계획하고 있지 않다. (We / a trip / are not / planning)

   ______________________________ .

5. 폴은 사진을 찍고 있지 않다. (pictures / taking / is not / Paul)

   ______________________________ .

A 영어는 우리말로, 우리말은 영어로 쓰세요.

❶ drive	______	⓫ 수영	______
❷ hard	______	⓬ 꽃	______
❸ cross	______	⓭ 자다	______
❹ ride	______	⓮ 쓰다	______
❺ sandwich	______	⓯ 전화기	______
❻ song	______	⓰ 파티	______
❼ homework	______	⓱ 야채	______
❽ kitchen	______	⓲ 테니스	______
❾ snowman	______	⓳ 택시	______
❿ art museum	______	⓴ 음악	______

B 괄호 안에서 알맞은 것을 고르세요.

❶ Is she (watch / watching) TV?

❷ Are (singing you / you singing) a song?

❸ (Do / Are) you washing the dishes?

❹ (Does / Is) he cooking dinner?

❺ Are you (write / writing) a novel?

❻ Is he (use / using) a telephone?

❼ Are the boys (make / making) a snowman?

❽ Is he (do / doing) his homework?

❾ Is she (having / have) breakfast?

❿ Is (he driving / driving he) a bus?

C 괄호 안에 주어진 단어를 이용해서 빈칸을 완성하세요.

1. ________ she ________ TV? (watching / Is)
2. ________ you ________ a song? (Are / singing)
3. ________ you ________ the dishes? (Are / washing)
4. ________ he ________ dinner? (cooking / Is)
5. ________ you ________ a novel? (writing / Are)
6. ________ he ________ a telephone? (Is / using)
7. ________ the boys ________ a snowman? (making / Are)
8. ________ he ________ his homework? (doing / Is)
9. ________ she ________ breakfast? (having / Is)
10. ________ he ________ a bus? (Is / driving)

D 우리말과 같도록 괄호 안의 말을 이용해서 문장을 완성하세요.

1. 그녀는 TV를 보고 있니? (she / watching / TV / Is)

____ ?

2. 너는 설거지를 하고 있니? (the dishes / Are / washing / you)

____ ?

3. 그는 전화기를 사용하고 있니? (using / he / Is / a telephone)

____ ?

4. 그 소년들은 눈사람을 만들고 있니? (the boys / making / a snowman / Are)

____ ?

5. 그는 버스를 운전하고 있니? (he / driving / Is / a bus)

____ ?

1	about	약, 대략	I am **about** 170cm. 나는 약 170cm이다.
2	address	주소	What is his **address**? 그의 주소는 무엇이니?
3	arrive	도착하다	When does he **arrive** here? 그는 언제 여기에 도착하니?
4	bridge	다리	How long is the **bridge**? 그 다리는 얼마나 기니?
5	building	빌딩, 건물	A man is coming out of the **building**. 남자가 그 빌딩에서 나오고 있다.
6	dream	꿈	What is Jenny's **dream**? 제니의 꿈은 무엇이니?
7	enjoy	즐기다	What sport do you **enjoy**? 너는 무슨 운동을 즐기니?
8	every Sunday	일요일마다	I go there **every Sunday**. 나는 일요일마다 거기에 간다.
9	far	먼	How **far** is it from here? 여기서 얼마나 머니?
10	favorite	가장 좋아하는	What is your **favorite** movie? 네가 가장 좋아하는 영화는 무엇이니?
11	feel	느끼다	How do you **feel**? 너는 기분이 어떠니?
12	hit	치다, 때리다	My brother never **hits** me. 나의 형은 결코 나를 때리지 않는다.
13	how	어떻게	**How** do you go to the store? 너는 그 가게에 어떻게 가니?
14	job	직업	What is your **job**? 너의 직업은 무엇이니?
15	know	알다	How does she **know** that? 그녀는 어떻게 그걸 아니?

16	**learn**	배우다	Why don't you **learn** English? 너는 영어를 배우는 게 어때?
17	**meeting**	회의	They have a **meeting** at noon. 그들은 정오에 회의가 있다.
18	**o'clock**	시, 정각	I go to bed at 10 **o'clock**. 나는 10시에 자러 간다.
19	**often**	자주, 종종	They **often** play basketball. 그들은 종종 농구를 한다.
20	**outside**	밖에	It is cold **outside**. 밖이 춥다.
21	**scold**	혼내다	Dad **scolds** me. 아빠가 나를 혼낸다.
22	**shower**	샤워	How often do you take a **shower**? 너는 얼마나 자주 샤워를 하니?
23	**spend**	(시간 등) 보내다	How do you **spend** your time? 너는 어떻게 시간을 보내니?
24	**under**	아래에	My book is **under** the bed. 나의 책은 침대 아래에 있다.
25	**weather**	날씨	How is the **weather**? 날씨는 어떠니?
26	**what**	무엇	**What** is your name? 너의 이름은 무엇이니?
27	**when**	언제	**When** is your birthday? 너의 생일은 언제니?
28	**where**	어디에	**Where** is your house? 너의 집은 어디니?
29	**who**	누구	**Who** are you? 너는 누구니?
30	**why**	왜	**Why** are you sad? 너는 왜 슬프니?

A 다음 우리말 뜻에 해당하는 영어 단어를 쓰세요.

❶ 약, 대략 → ____________________

❷ 시, 정각 → ____________________

❸ 자주, 종종 → ____________________

❹ 빌딩, 건물 → ____________________

❺ 치다, 때리다 → ____________________

❻ (시간 등) 보내다 → ____________________

❼ 언제 → ____________________

❽ 왜 → ____________________

❾ 어떻게 → ____________________

❿ 어디에 → ____________________

⓫ 꿈 → ____________________

⓬ 배우다 → ____________________

⓭ 날씨 → ____________________

⓮ 주소 → ____________________

⓯ 먼 → ____________________

/30

B 다음 영어 단어에 해당하는 우리말 뜻을 쓰세요.

❶ know → ______

❷ meeting → ______

❸ bridge → ______

❹ feel → ______

❺ job → ______

❻ enjoy → ______

❼ arrive → ______

❽ scold → ______

❾ shower → ______

❿ under → ______

⓫ favorite → ______

⓬ who → ______

⓭ outside → ______

⓮ what → ______

⓯ every Sunday → ______

A 영어는 우리말로, 우리말은 영어로 쓰세요.

① name	______	⑪ 부모	______
② birthday	______	⑫ 화난	______
③ house	______	⑬ 돕다	______
④ weather	______	⑭ 도착하다	______
⑤ invite	______	⑮ 시험	______
⑥ address	______	⑯ 오늘	______
⑦ know	______	⑰ 아래에	______
⑧ get up	______	⑱ 늦은, 늦게	______
⑨ live	______	⑲ 좋아하는	______
⑩ leave	______	⑳ 전화번호	______

B 괄호 안에서 알맞은 것을 고르세요.

① A: (Why / When) is the test? B: It is June 3rd.

② A: (When / What) do you like? B: I like reading.

③ A: (How / When) are you today? B: I am fine.

④ A: (Who / Why) are you sad? B: Because my cat is sick.

⑤ A: (Where / How) is my book? B: It is under the bed.

⑥ A: (Who / What) is that woman? B: She is my sister.

⑦ (What / Where) is my book?

⑧ (When / What) is his phone number?

⑨ (How / When) is Jenny's birthday?

⑩ (Why / Where) are you angry?

C 괄호 안에 주어진 단어를 이용해서 빈칸을 완성하세요.

1. A: ________ is the test? B: It is ____________. (When / June 3rd)
2. A: ________ do you like? B: I like ____________. (reading / What)
3. A: ________ are you today? B: I am ____________. (How / fine)
4. A: ________ are you sad? B: __________ my cat is sick. (Because / Why)
5. A: ________ is my book? B: It is ___________ the bed. (Where / under)
6. A: ________ is that woman? B: She is ___________. (Who / my sister)
7. ______________ is ______________? (Where / my book)
8. ______________ is his ______________? (What / phone number)
9. ______________ is ______________? (Jenny's birthday / When)
10. ______________ are you ______________? (angry / Why)

D 우리말과 같도록 괄호 안의 말을 이용해서 문장을 완성하세요.

1. 너는 무엇을 좋아하니? (What / like / do you)

   ____ ?

2. 내 책은 어디 있니? (my book / Where / is)

   ____ ?

3. 너는 오늘 어떠니? (are / you / How / today)

   ____ ?

4. 제니의 생일은 언제니? (Jenny's birthday / When / is)

   ____ ?

5. 너는 왜 슬프니? (sad / are / you / Why)

   ____ ?

A 영어는 우리말로, 우리말은 영어로 쓰세요.

❶ color	________	⓫ 공부하다	________
❷ friend	________	⓬ 숙녀	________
❸ dream	________	⓭ 즐기다	________
❹ sister	________	⓮ 함께 가다	________
❺ choose	________	⓯ 여자	________
❻ sport	________	⓰ 머리카락	________
❼ need	________	⓱ 음식	________
❽ son	________	⓲ 마시다	________
❾ help	________	⓳ 누구	________
❿ meet	________	⓴ 무엇	________

B 괄호 안에서 알맞은 것을 고르세요.

❶ A: (Who / What) is your brother? B: Tom is my brother.

❷ A: (Who / What) is his name? B: His name is Jack.

❸ A: (What color / Who) do you like? B: I like blue.

❹ A: (What / Who) is this? B: It's a ball.

❺ A: (Who / What) are these? B: They are kiwis.

❻ (Who / What) is their son?

❼ (Who / What) is your favorite movie?

❽ (Who / What) does she drink?

❾ (Who / What) is this girl?

❿ (What book / Who) do you read?

C 괄호 안에 주어진 단어를 이용해서 빈칸을 완성하세요.

1. A: ________ is your brother? B: Tom is ____________. (my brother / Who)
2. A: ________ is his name? B: His name is ____________. (What / Jack)
3. A: ________ do you like? B: I like ____________. (blue / What color)
4. A: ________ is this? B: It's ____________. (What / a ball)
5. A: ________ are these? B: They are ____________. (kiwis / What)
6. ____________ is ____________________? (Who / their son)
7. ____________ is your ____________________? (favorite movie / What)
8. ____________ does she ____________________? (drink / What)
9. ____________ is ____________________? (this girl / Who)
10. ____________ do you ____________________? (What book / read)

D 우리말과 같도록 괄호 안의 말을 이용해서 문장을 완성하세요.

1. 그의 이름은 무엇이니? (his name / What / is)

   ____?

2. 이 소녀는 누구니? (is / this girl / Who)

   ____?

3. 너는 무슨 책을 읽니? (What book / read / do you)

   ____?

4. 그녀는 무엇을 마시니? (What / does she / drink)

   ____?

5. 이것들은 무엇이니? (What / these / are)

   ____?

A 영어는 우리말로, 우리말은 영어로 쓰세요.

1. when ____________
2. where ____________
3. live ____________
4. o'clock ____________
5. test ____________
6. bookstore ____________
7. breakfast ____________
8. notebook ____________
9. meeting ____________
10. take a walk ____________
11. 팔다 ____________
12. 타다 ____________
13. 가로질러 ____________
14. 도서관 ____________
15. 크리스마스 ____________
16. 아이들 ____________
17. 저녁, 저녁 식사 ____________
18. 병원 ____________
19. 농구 ____________
20. 경찰서 ____________

B 괄호 안에서 알맞은 것을 고르세요.

1. A: (Where / When) do you live? B: I live in Seoul.
2. A: (Where / When) is your birthday? B: It's July 1st.
3. A: (Where / When) do you eat breakfast? B: I eat breakfast at 7.
4. A: (Where / When) is the library? B: It's across the street.
5. A: (What time / Where) do you go to bed? B: I go to bed at 11.
6. (When / Where) is Parents' Day?
7. (When / Where) does Jack live?
8. (When / Where) is Children's Day?
9. (When / Where) are the children?
10. (When / Where) are your notebooks?

C 괄호 안에 주어진 단어를 이용해서 빈칸을 완성하세요.

1. A: ________ do you live? B: I live ____________. (in Seoul / Where)
2. A: ________ is your birthday? B: It's ____________. (July 1st / When)
3. A: ______ do you eat breakfast? B: I eat breakfast ________. (When / at 7)
4. A: ______ is the library? B: It's across ____________. (Where / the street)
5. A: ______ do you go to bed? B: I go to bed ________. (at 11 / What time)
6. ______ is ________________? (When / Parents' Day)
7. ______ does Jack ________________? (live / Where)
8. ________ is ____________________? (When / Children's Day)
9. ________ are ____________________? (the children / Where)
10. ____________ are ______________________? (your notebook / Where)

D 우리말과 같도록 괄호 안의 말을 이용해서 문장을 완성하세요.

1. 너는 언제 아침을 먹니? (When / breakfast / eat / do you)

   ____ ?

2. 잭은 어디에 사니? (live / does Jack / Where)

   ____ ?

3. 어린이 날은 언제니? (When / Children's Day / is)

   ____ ?

4. 그 아이들은 어디 있니? (are / Where / the children)

   ____ ?

5. 너는 몇 시에 자러 가니? (go to bed / What time / do you)

   ____ ?

A 영어는 우리말로, 우리말은 영어로 쓰세요.

❶ why ____________
❷ how ____________
❸ late ____________
❹ learn ____________
❺ stay ____________
❻ because ____________
❼ hit ____________
❽ angry ____________
❾ expensive ____________
❿ hate ____________
⓫ 느끼다 ____________
⓬ 바쁜 ____________
⓭ 가게, 상점 ____________
⓮ 걱정하다 ____________
⓯ 날씨 ____________
⓰ 울다 ____________
⓱ 혼내다 ____________
⓲ (시간 등) 보내다 ____________
⓳ 시간 ____________
⓴ 밖에 ____________

B 괄호 안에서 알맞은 것을 고르세요.

❶ A: (How / Why) do you feel today? B: I feel good.
❷ A: (How / Why) do they stay at home? B: Because it's cold outside.
❸ A: (How / Why) is this music? B: It sounds good.
❹ A: (How / Why) are they so happy? B: Because they win the game.
❺ A: (How / Why) does he go to work? B: He goes to work by car.
❻ (How / Why) don't you learn English?
❼ (How / Why) are you angry?
❽ (How / Why) is the new car?
❾ (How / Why) do you worry so much?
❿ (How / Why) is the weather today?

C 괄호 안에 주어진 단어를 이용해서 빈칸을 완성하세요.

1. A: ________ do you feel today? B: I feel ________. (good / How)
2. A: ______ do they stay at home? B: _______ it's cold outside. (Because / Why)
3. A: ______ is this music? B: It sounds ________. (How / good)
4. A: ______ are they so happy? B: _______ they win the game. (Why / Because)
5. A: ______ does he go to work? B: He goes to work ________. (How / by car)
6. ______________________________ English? (Why don't you / learn)
7. ___________ are you ___________________? (Why / angry)
8. ___________ is ___________________? (the new car / How)
9. ___________ do you ___________________ so much? (worry / Why)
10. ___________ is ___________________ today? (the weather / How)

D 우리말과 같도록 괄호 안의 말을 이용해서 문장을 완성하세요.

1. 이 음악은 어때? (is / this music / How)

   ____?

2. 그들은 왜 집에 머물고 있니? (stay home / do they / Why)

   ____?

3. 너는 왜 화가 났니? (are / you / Why / angry)

   ____?

4. 영어를 배우는 게 어때? (Why don't you / English / learn)

   ____?

5. 오늘 날씨는 어떠니? (is / today / How / the weather)

   ____?

A 영어는 우리말로, 우리말은 영어로 쓰세요.

1. about ________
2. meter ________
3. kilometer ________
4. every day ________
5. often ________
6. building ________
7. far ________
8. post office ________
9. library ________
10. river ________
11. 다리 ________
12. 은행 ________
13. 운동하다 ________
14. 바구니 ________
15. 빵 ________
16. 언덕 ________
17. 샤워 ________
18. 교실 ________
19. 영화 ________
20. 토요일마다 ________

B 괄호 안에서 알맞은 것을 고르세요.

1. A: (How old / How far) are you? B: I'm 12 years old.
2. A: (How long / How often) is the snake? B: It's about 2 meters long.
3. A: (How often / How tall) is he? B: He's about 150cm.
4. How (many / much) water is in the glass?
5. How (many / much) pencils do you have?
6. (How far / How long) is your house from here?
7. (How old / How often) do you take a shower?
8. How (many / much) books do you have?
9. How (many / much) sugar does she buy?
10. (How often / How far) does she play the piano?

C 괄호 안에 주어진 단어를 이용해서 빈칸을 완성하세요.

1. A: ______________ are you? B: I'm 12 years old. (How / old)
2. A: ______________ is the snake? B: It's about 2 meters long. (long / How)
3. A: ______________ is he? B: He's about 150cm. (How / tall)
4. ______________ water is in the glass? (much / How)
5. ______________ pencils do you have? (many / How)
6. ______________ is your house from here? (How / far)
7. ______________ do you take a shower? (How / often)
8. ______________ books do you have? (How / many)
9. ______________ sugar does she buy? (much / How)
10. ______________ does she play the piano? (often / How)

D 우리말과 같도록 괄호 안의 말을 이용해서 문장을 완성하세요.

1. 너는 몇 살이니? (are / you / How old)

   ______________________________________?

2. 그녀는 얼마나 많은 설탕을 사니? (buy / How much / sugar / does she)

   ______________________________________?

3. 너는 얼마나 많은 책을 가지고 있니? (books / How many / do you / have)

   ______________________________________?

4. 그녀는 얼마나 자주 피아노를 치니? (How often / play the piano / does she)

   ______________________________________?

5. 그 뱀은 얼마나 기니? (is / How long / the snake)

   ______________________________________?

1	**after**	후에	I play games **after** I eat dinner. 나는 저녁을 먹은 후에 게임을 한다.
2	**always**	언제나	You are **always** late for school. 너는 항상 학교에 지각한다.
3	**because**	때문에	Jack likes her **because** she is kind. 잭은 그녀가 친절하기 때문에 그녀를 좋아한다.
4	**before**	전에	He reads a book **before** he goes to sleep. 그는 자러 가기 전에 책을 읽는다.
5	**cheap**	싼	This bag is nice but **cheap**. 이 가방은 멋지지만 싸다.
6	**choose**	고르다	You can **choose** black or white. 너는 검정색이나 하얀색을 고를 수 있다.
7	**concert**	콘서트	I often go to **concerts**. 나는 종종 콘서트에 간다.
8	**finish**	마치다	I watch TV after I **finish** my homework. 나는 숙제를 끝낸 후에 TV를 본다.
9	**funny**	재미있는	My teacher is kind and **funny**. 나의 선생님은 친절하고 재미있다.
10	**handsome**	잘생긴	Bill is **handsome** and kind. 빌은 잘생기고 친절하다.
11	**healthy**	건강한	My grandfather is old but **healthy**. 나의 할아버지는 나이 들었지만 건강하다.
12	**knock**	노크하다	I open the door after I **knock** the door. 나는 노크를 한 후에 문을 연다.
13	**laugh**	웃다	They **laugh** because they are happy. 그들은 행복하기 때문에 웃는다.
14	**lazy**	게으른	He doesn't clean because he is **lazy**. 그는 게으르기 때문에 청소하지 않는다.
15	**left**	왼쪽	You can turn **left** or right. 너는 왼쪽 또는 오른쪽으로 돌 수 있다.

16	listen	듣다	He **listens** to music every day. 그는 매일 음악을 듣는다.
17	news	소식, 뉴스	The **news** is surprising. 그 소식은 놀랍다.
18	newspaper	신문	She reads the **newspaper** in the morning. 그녀는 아침에 신문을 읽는다.
19	office	사무실	My uncle is at home or at the **office**. 나의 삼촌은 집 또는 사무실에 있다.
20	photo	사진	I have her **photos**. 난 그녀의 사진들을 가지고 있다.
21	plane	비행기	The **plane** is fast and safe. 그 비행기는 빠르고 안전하다.
22	poor	가난한	I am **poor** but happy. 나는 가난하지만 행복하다.
23	right	오른쪽	Turn **right** at the corner. 모퉁이에서 오른쪽으로 돌아라.
24	safely	안전하게	My car runs fast and **safely**. 나의 자동차는 빠르고 안전하게 달린다.
25	sick	아픈	Mary is **sick**, so she goes to the doctor. 메리는 아파서 병원에 간다.
26	so	그래서	He is angry, **so** he speaks loudly. 그는 화가 나서 크게 말한다.
27	subway	지하철	We go to school by **subway**. 우리는 지하철을 타고 학교에 간다.
28	true	사실인	The news is sad but **true**. 그 소식은 슬프지만 사실이다.
29	wear	입다	She is **wearing** a dress. 그녀는 드레스를 입고 있다.
30	young	젊은	Anna is **young** and beautiful. 애나는 젊고 아름답다.

A 다음 우리말 뜻에 해당하는 영어 단어를 쓰세요.

❶ 전에 → ______

❷ 후에 → ______

❸ 소식, 뉴스 → ______

❹ 고르다 → ______

❺ 지하철 → ______

❻ 재미있는 → ______

❼ 그래서 → ______

❽ 때문에 → ______

❾ 왼쪽 → ______

❿ 콘서트 → ______

⓫ 마치다 → ______

⓬ 가난한 → ______

⓭ 오른쪽 → ______

⓮ 신문 → ______

⓯ 젊은 → ______

B 다음 영어 단어에 해당하는 우리말 뜻을 쓰세요.

1. safely → ______________________
2. wear → ______________________
3. always → ______________________
4. healthy → ______________________
5. listen → ______________________
6. true → ______________________
7. photo → ______________________
8. cheap → ______________________
9. lazy → ______________________
10. knock → ______________________
11. plane → ______________________
12. handsome → ______________________
13. sick → ______________________
14. laugh → ______________________
15. office → ______________________

A 영어는 우리말로, 우리말은 영어로 쓰세요.

❶ choose ______

❷ subway ______

❸ funny ______

❹ left ______

❺ black ______

❻ white ______

❼ poor ______

❽ right ______

❾ strong ______

❿ young ______

⓫ 안전하게 ______

⓬ (과일) 배 ______

⓭ 건강한 ______

⓮ 사실인 ______

⓯ 비싼 ______

⓰ 싼 ______

⓱ 소식, 뉴스 ______

⓲ 비행기 ______

⓳ 잘생긴 ______

⓴ 사무실 ______

B 괄호 안에서 알맞은 것을 고르세요.

❶ 너는 연필과 공책을 가지고 있다. You have pencils (and / but) notebooks.

❷ 엄마와 아빠는 산책을 한다. Mom (and / or) Dad take a walk.

❸ 그들은 집에 있거나 학교에 있다. They are at home (or / and) at school.

❹ 그 드레스는 검은색 또는 하얀색이다. The dress is black (or / but) white.

❺ 너와 나는 좋은 친구다. You (and / but) I are good friends.

❻ 그는 나이가 들었지만 건강하다. He is old (or / but) healthy.

❼ 엄마나 아빠가 집에 있다. There is Mom (but / or) Dad at home.

❽ 그녀는 가난하지만 행복하다. She is poor (and / but) happy.

❾ 이 가방은 멋지지만 비싸다. This bag is nice (and / but) cheap.

❿ 그는 아침으로 빵과 우유를 먹는다. He eats bread (and / but) milk for breakfast.

C 괄호 안에 주어진 단어를 이용해서 빈칸을 완성하세요.

1. You have ______________________. (pencils / and notebooks)
2. ______________________ take a walk. (and Dad / Mom)
3. They are ______________________. (at home / or at school)
4. The dress is ______________________. (or white / black)
5. ______________________ are good friends. (You / and I)
6. He is ______________________. (but healthy / old)
7. There is ______________________ at home. (Mom / or Dad)
8. She is ______________________. (poor / but happy)
9. This bag is ______________________. (and cheap / nice)
10. He eats ______________________ for breakfast. (bread / and milk)

D 우리말과 같도록 괄호 안의 말을 이용해서 문장을 완성하세요.

1. 너는 연필과 공책을 가지고 있다. (You / pencils / notebooks / and / have)

   ____.

2. 그 드레스는 검정색 또는 하얀색이다. (The dress / white / black / or / is)

   ____.

3. 그녀는 가난하지만 행복하다. (but / She / is / poor / happy)

   ____.

4. 너와 나는 좋은 친구다. (You / and / I / good friends / are)

   ____.

5. 그는 나이가 들었지만 건강하다. (old / He / healthy / but / is)

   ____.

A 영어는 우리말로, 우리말은 영어로 쓰세요.

① before	________	⑪ 일어나다	________
② after	________	⑫ 입다	________
③ so	________	⑬ 언제나	________
④ because	________	⑭ 듣다	________
⑤ concert	________	⑮ 사진	________
⑥ sleep	________	⑯ 카메라	________
⑦ finish	________	⑰ 게으른	________
⑧ go out	________	⑱ 노크하다	________
⑨ solve	________	⑲ 아픈	________
⑩ newspaper	________	⑳ 웃다	________

B 괄호 안에서 알맞은 것을 고르세요.

① You watch TV (after / so) you finish your homework.

② We are happy, (so / because) we smile.

③ I open the door (because / after) I knock the door.

④ He doesn't clean his room (before / because) he is lazy.

⑤ We can't go to the party (so / because) we are busy.

⑥ He is angry, (so / after) he speaks loudly.

⑦ My sister drinks milk (because / before) she goes to bed.

⑧ I brush my teeth (so / after) I eat breakfast.

⑨ I can't go out (after / because) it's raining.

⑩ David is sick, (so / because) he can't go to school.

C 괄호 안에 주어진 단어를 이용해서 빈칸을 완성하세요.

1. You watch TV ________________ your homework. (after / you finish)
2. We are happy, ________________. (we smile / so)
3. I open the door ________________ the door. (after / I knock)
4. He doesn't clean his room ________________. (he is lazy / because)
5. We can't go to the party ________________. (we are busy / because)
6. He is angry, ________________ loudly. (so / he speaks)
7. My sister drinks milk ________________. (she goes to bed / before)
8. I brush my teeth ________________. (after / I eat breakfast)
9. I can't go out ________________. (it's raining / because)
10. David is sick, ________________ to school. (so / he can't go)

D 우리말과 같도록 괄호 안의 말을 이용해서 문장을 완성하세요.

1. 나는 노크를 한 후에 문을 연다. (I / after / open the door / knock the door)

   I ________________________________ .

2. 내 여동생은 자러 가기 전에 우유를 마신다. (drinks milk / goes to bed / before / she)

   My sister ________________________________ .

3. 비가 오기 때문에 나는 외출할 수가 없다. (it's / can't go out / raining / because)

   I ________________________________ .

4. 데이비드는 아파서 학교에 갈 수 없다. (so / is sick / go to school / he can't)

   David ________________________________ .

5. 나는 아침을 먹고 난 후에 이를 닦는다. (brush my teeth / eat breakfast / after / I)

   I ________________________________ .

1	**bake**	굽다	Let's **bake** cookies. 쿠키를 굽자.
2	**beach**	해변	Let's not go to the **beach**. 해변에 가지 말자.
3	**brave**	용감한	How **brave** he is! 그는 정말 용감하구나
4	**careful**	조심하는	Be **careful**. 조심해라.
5	**close**	닫다	Don't **close** the door. 문을 닫지 마라.
6	**computer**	컴퓨터	The children play **computer** games. 그 아이들은 컴퓨터 게임을 한다.
7	**cute**	귀여운	I know a **cute** baby. 나는 귀여운 아기를 안다.
8	**difficult**	어려운	What a **difficult** problem! 정말 어려운 문제구나!
9	**dirty**	더러운	The bag is very **dirty**. 그 가방은 매우 더럽다.
10	**eat out**	외식하다	Let's **eat out** together. 함께 외식하자.
11	**fail**	실패하다	Study hard, or you will **fail** the test. 열심히 공부해라, 그렇지 않으면 그 시험에 떨어질 것이다.
12	**famous**	유명한	He is a very **famous** actor. 그는 매우 유명한 배우다.
13	**fat**	뚱뚱한	Look at the **fat** cat. 그 뚱뚱한 고양이를 봐라.
14	**heavy**	무거운	He is moving a **heavy** box. 그는 무거운 상자를 옮기고 있다.
15	**hurry up**	서두르다	**Hurry up**, and you will catch the bus. 서둘러라, 그러면 버스를 잡을 것이다.

16	**jog**	조깅하다	**Jog** every day, and you will be healthy. 매일 조깅을 해라, 그러면 건강해질 것이다.
17	**light**	불, 빛	Please turn off the **light**. 불을 꺼주세요.
18	**please**	부디, 제발	Stand up, **please**. (제발) 일어서 주세요.
19	**pretty**	예쁜	The house has a **pretty** garden. 그 집은 예쁜 정원이 있다.
20	**restaurant**	식당, 레스토랑	They are going to the **restaurant**. 그들은 레스토랑에 가고 있다.
21	**smart**	똑똑한	Read many books, and you will be **smart**. 책을 많이 읽어라, 그러면 똑똑해질 것이다.
22	**snowman**	눈사람	Let's make a **snowman**. 눈사람을 만들자.
23	**stand up**	일어서다	It helps you **stand up**. 그것은 너가 일어서도록 돕는다.
24	**story**	이야기	I know a beautiful **story**. 나는 아름다운 이야기를 안다.
25	**thick**	두꺼운	The girl is carrying a **thick** book. 그 소녀는 두꺼운 책을 들고 있다.
26	**thin**	마른	The doll has a **thin** body. 그 인형은 마른 몸을 하고 있다.
27	**touch**	만지다	Let's not **touch** the dog. 그 개를 만지지 말자.
28	**turn off**	끄다	You must **turn off** the light. 너는 불을 꺼야 한다.
29	**turn on**	켜다	I always **turn on** the TV. 나는 항상 TV를 켠다.
30	**wise**	현명한	How **wise** she is! 그녀는 정말 현명하구나!

A 다음 우리말 뜻에 해당하는 영어 단어를 쓰세요.

❶ 부디, 제발 ⟶ ____________________

❷ 식당, 레스토랑 ⟶ ____________________

❸ 불, 빛 ⟶ ____________________

❹ 귀여운 ⟶ ____________________

❺ 해변 ⟶ ____________________

❻ 똑똑한 ⟶ ____________________

❼ 예쁜 ⟶ ____________________

❽ 용감한 ⟶ ____________________

❾ 조깅하다 ⟶ ____________________

❿ 뚱뚱한 ⟶ ____________________

⓫ 굽다 ⟶ ____________________

⓬ 닫다 ⟶ ____________________

⓭ 조심하는 ⟶ ____________________

⓮ 마른 ⟶ ____________________

⓯ 어려운 ⟶ ____________________

/30

B 다음 영어 단어에 해당하는 우리말 뜻을 쓰세요.

1. snowman → ____________________
2. story → ____________________
3. famous → ____________________
4. touch → ____________________
5. dirty → ____________________
6. computer → ____________________
7. wise → ____________________
8. thick → ____________________
9. fail → ____________________
10. heavy → ____________________
11. eat out → ____________________
12. stand up → ____________________
13. turn off → ____________________
14. hurry up → ____________________
15. turn on → ____________________

A 영어는 우리말로, 우리말은 영어로 쓰세요.

❶ open	________	⓫ 일어서다	________
❷ window	________	⓬ 만지다	________
❸ quiet	________	⓭ 불, 빛	________
❹ please	________	⓮ 끄다	________
❺ jog	________	⓯ 서두르다	________
❻ healthy	________	⓰ 배고픈	________
❼ wake up	________	⓱ 실패하다	________
❽ close	________	⓲ 통과하다	________
❾ careful	________	⓳ 켜다	________
❿ brush	________	⓴ 잡다	________

B 괄호 안에서 알맞은 것을 고르세요.

❶ (Be / Am) a good girl.

❷ (Goes / Go) to the park.

❸ (Don't / Doesn't) stand up.

❹ (Brush / Brushes) your teeth.

❺ (Goes / Go) to bed early.

❻ (Doesn't / Don't) run in the classroom.

❼ (Do / Does) your homework first.

❽ Jog every day, (and / or) you will be healthy.

❾ Hurry up, (and / or) you will be late for school.

❿ Push the button, (and / or) the door will open.

C 괄호 안에 주어진 단어를 이용해서 빈칸을 완성하세요.

1. ______________ a good ______________. (Be / girl)
2. ______________ to the ______________. (park / Go)
3. __________________________ up. (stand / Don't)
4. ______________ your ______________. (Brush / teeth)
5. __________________________ early. (Go / to bed)
6. __________________________ in the classroom. (run / Don't)
7. __________________________ first. (Do / your homework)
8. Jog every day, ______________________ be healthy. (and / you will)
9. Hurry up, ______________________ be late for school. (or / you will)
10. Push the button, ______________________ open. (the door will / and)

D 우리말과 같도록 괄호 안의 말을 이용해서 문장을 완성하세요.

1. 공원으로 가라. (to / the park / Go)

   ____.

2. 교실에서 뛰지 마라. (run / in the classroom / Don't)

   ____.

3. 숙제 먼저 해라. (Do / your homework / first)

   ____.

4. 매일 조깅을 해라, 그러면 건강해질 것이다. (and / will / be healthy / you)

   Jog every day, ____.

5. 서둘러라, 그렇지 않으면 학교에 늦을 것이다. (or / will / you / for school / be late)

   Hurry up, ____.

A 영어는 우리말로, 우리말은 영어로 쓰세요.

❶ let's	______	⓫ 먼저	______
❷ beach	______	⓬ 앉다	______
❸ buy	______	⓭ 휴식	______
❹ kid	______	⓮ 점심, 점심 식사	______
❺ eat out	______	⓯ 컴퓨터	______
❻ together	______	⓰ 사진	______
❼ library	______	⓱ 자전거	______
❽ bake	______	⓲ 티셔츠	______
❾ vegetable	______	⓳ 박물관	______
❿ snowman	______	⓴ 청소하다	______

B 괄호 안에서 알맞은 것을 고르세요.

❶ Let's (reads / read) a book.

❷ Let's (go / goes) to the library.

❸ Why don't we (go / goes) to the park?

❹ Why don't we (takes / take) a rest here?

❺ (Not let's / Let's not) go to the beach.

❻ Let's (sit not / not sit) on the bench.

❼ Let's (not watch / watch not) the movie.

❽ Let's (drink / drinks) water

❾ (Not let's / Let's not) take pictures here.

❿ Let's (make / makes) a snowman.

C 괄호 안에 주어진 단어를 이용해서 빈칸을 완성하세요.

1. ________________ a book. (read / Let's)
2. ________________ to the library. (Let's / go)
3. ________________ to the park? (go / Why don't we)
4. ________________ a rest here? (take / Why don't we)
5. ________________ to the beach. (Let's not / go)
6. ________________ on the bench. (Let's not / sit)
7. ________________ the movie. (watch / Let's not)
8. ________________ water. (Let's / drink)
9. ________________ pictures here. (take / Let's not)
10. ________________ a snowman. (Let's / make)

D 우리말과 같도록 괄호 안의 말을 이용해서 문장을 완성하세요.

1. 책을 읽자. (read / a book / Let's)

   ________________________________ .

2. 해변에 가지 말자. (Let's / to the beach / not / go)

   ________________________________ .

3. 공원에 가는 게 어때? (to the park / go / Why don't we)

   ________________________________ ?

4. 여기서 사진을 찍지 말자. (Let's / here / not / take pictures)

   ________________________________ .

5. 눈사람을 만들자. (make / a snowman / Let's)

   ________________________________ .

A 영어는 우리말로, 우리말은 영어로 쓰세요.

1. cute ____________
2. smart ____________
3. pretty ____________
4. brave ____________
5. restaurant ____________
6. fat ____________
7. busy ____________
8. handsome ____________
9. thin ____________
10. difficult ____________
11. 이야기 ____________
12. 유명한 ____________
13. 더러운 ____________
14. 비싼 ____________
15. 현명한 ____________
16. 두꺼운 ____________
17. 재미, 재미있는 ____________
18. 어린, 젊은 ____________
19. 무거운 ____________
20. 싼 ____________

B 괄호 안에서 알맞은 것을 고르세요.

1. (How / What) kind you are!
2. (How / What) a smart girl!
3. (How / What) strong he is!
4. (How / What) a beautiful picture!
5. How (lazy she / she lazy) is!
6. What (pretty a / a pretty) garden!
7. How fast (are you / you are)!
8. What (a dirty / dirty a) room!
9. How long (the snake is / is the snake)!
10. How busy (your dad is / is your dad)!

C 괄호 안에 주어진 단어를 이용해서 빈칸을 완성하세요.

1. ______________________ you are! (How / kind)
2. ______________________ girl! (a smart / What)
3. ______________________ he is! (strong / How)
4. ______________________ picture! (What / a beautiful)
5. ______________________ she is! (lazy / How)
6. What ______________________! (garden / a pretty)
7. ______________________ you are! (How / fast)
8. What ______________________! (a dirty / room)
9. How long ______________________! (the snake / is)
10. How busy ______________________! (is / your dad)

D 우리말과 같도록 괄호 안의 말을 이용해서 문장을 완성하세요.

1. 너는 정말 친절하구나! (How / are / kind / you)

   ____!

2. 정말 예쁜 정원이구나! (garden / a pretty / What)

   ____!

3. 너희 아빠는 정말 바쁘구나! (your dad / How / busy / is)

   ____!

4. 정말 더러운 방이구나! (a dirty / What / room)

   ____!

5. 그녀는 정말 게으르구나! (How / is / she / lazy)

   ____!

1	**basket**	바구니	There are ten apples in the **basket**. 바구니 안에 사과 열 개가 있다.
2	**birthday**	생일	Today is my eleventh **birthday**. 오늘은 나의 열한 번째 생일이다.
3	**cent**	센트	This pen is eighty **cents**. 이 펜은 80센트다.
4	**dollar**	달러	These shoes are twenty-five **dollars**. 이 신발들은 25달러다.
5	**February**	2월	Today is Monday, **February** seventh. 오늘은 2월 7일 월요일이다.
6	**fifth**	다섯 번째	Children's Day is May the **fifth**. 어린이날은 5월 5일이다.
7	**floor**	마루, 층	His office is on the thirtieth **floor**. 그의 사무실은 30층이다.
8	**fourth**	네 번째	The day after tomorrow is May **fourth**. 모레는 5월 4일이다.
9	**front**	앞	There are people in **front** of the building. 건물 앞에 사람들이 있다.
10	**garden**	정원	There are ten trees in the **garden**. 정원에는 열 그루의 나무가 있다.
11	**grade**	학년	My brother is in the fifth **grade**. 나의 남동생은 5학년이다.
12	**guest**	손님	He is the hundredth **guest**. 그는 백 번째 손님이다.
13	**hundred**	백, 100	There are one **hundred** stars in the sky. 하늘에 100개의 별이 있다.
14	**line**	선, 줄	Jack is the tenth in **line**. 잭은 줄에서 열 번째 있다.
15	**month**	달, 월	March is the third **month**. 3월은 세 번째 달이다.

16	**ninth**	아홉 번째	He lives on the **ninth** floor. 그는 9층에 산다.
17	**number**	번호, 전화번호	My **number** is 535-8743. 나의 전화번호는 535-8743이다.
18	**people**	사람들	There are many **people** in the park. 공원에 많은 사람들이 있다.
19	**playground**	운동장	There are students on the **playground**. 운동장에 학생들이 있다.
20	**pocket**	주머니	I have coins in my **pocket**. 난 주머니에 동전이 있다.
21	**second**	두 번째	Amy is the **second** child. 에이미는 두 번째 아이다.
22	**series**	시리즈	I read the second book of the **series**. 나는 그 시리즈의 두 번째 책을 읽는다.
23	**shoes**	신발	These **shoes** fit me. 이 신발들은 나에게 잘 맞는다.
24	**third**	세 번째	The **third** man is my father. 세 번째 남자가 나의 아빠다.
25	**thousand**	천, 1000	There are twelve **thousand** students in the school. 학교에는 12,000명의 학생들이 있다.
26	**today**	오늘	I get up early **today**. 나는 오늘 일찍 일어난다.
27	**toy car**	장난감 자동차	My brother buys a new **toy car**. 나의 남동생은 새 장난감 자동차를 산다.
28	**visitor**	방문객	She is the thirteenth **visitor**. 그녀는 열세 번째 방문객이다.
29	**year**	해, 연	This is the **year** 2017. 올해는 2017년이다.
30	**zero**	0, 제로	My password is eight three four **zero**. 나의 비밀번호는 8340이다.

A **다음 우리말 뜻에 해당하는 영어 단어를 쓰세요.**

❶ 천, 1000 ⟶ ________________

❷ 다섯 번째 ⟶ ________________

❸ 백, 100 ⟶ ________________

❹ 0, 제로 ⟶ ________________

❺ 번호, 전화번호 ⟶ ________________

❻ 선, 줄 ⟶ ________________

❼ 마루, 층 ⟶ ________________

❽ 해, 연 ⟶ ________________

❾ 달, 월 ⟶ ________________

❿ 달러 ⟶ ________________

⓫ 두 번째 ⟶ ________________

⓬ 센트 ⟶ ________________

⓭ 세 번째 ⟶ ________________

⓮ 네 번째 ⟶ ________________

⓯ 아홉 번째 ⟶ ________________

/30

B 다음 영어 단어에 해당하는 우리말 뜻을 쓰세요.

1. shoes → ____________
2. playground → ____________
3. birthday → ____________
4. garden → ____________
5. people → ____________
6. series → ____________
7. grade → ____________
8. guest → ____________
9. front → ____________
10. today → ____________
11. February → ____________
12. visitor → ____________
13. basket → ____________
14. pocket → ____________
15. toy car → ____________

A 영어는 우리말로, 우리말은 영어로 쓰세요.

❶ first	______	⓫ 정원	______
❷ second	______	⓬ 마루, 층	______
❸ third	______	⓭ 달, 월	______
❹ fourth	______	⓮ 시리즈	______
❺ fifth	______	⓯ 학년	______
❻ ninth	______	⓰ 손님	______
❼ hundred	______	⓱ 잔디, 풀	______
❽ twentieth	______	⓲ 방문객	______
❾ birthday	______	⓳ 바구니	______
❿ line	______	⓴ 주머니	______

B 괄호 안에서 알맞은 것을 고르세요.

❶ There are (three / third) balls.

❷ Jack is the (ten / tenth) in line.

❸ I have (three / third) brothers.

❹ Today is his (forty / fortieth) birthday.

❺ (Seven / Seventh) birds fly in the sky.

❻ He lives on the (sixteen / sixteenth) floor.

❼ I read the (two / second) book of the series.

❽ He is the (hundred / hundredth) guest.

❾ November is the (eleven / eleventh) month.

❿ There are (eight / eighth) coins.

C 괄호 안에 주어진 단어를 이용해서 빈칸을 완성하세요.

1. There are ______________________. (three / balls)
2. Jack is the ______________________. (in line / tenth)
3. I have ______________________. (brothers / three)
4. Today is his ______________________. (fortieth / birthday)
5. ______________________ fly in the sky. (birds / Seven)
6. He lives on the ______________________. (sixteenth / floor)
7. I read the ______________________ of the series. (book / second)
8. He is the ______________________. (hundredth / guest)
9. November is the ______________________. (month / eleventh)
10. There are ______________________. (eight / coins)

D 우리말과 같도록 괄호 안의 말을 이용해서 문장을 완성하세요.

1. 3개의 공이 있다. (There / balls / three / are)

   ____.

2. 오늘은 그의 마흔 번째 생일이다. (is / his fortieth / birthday / Today)

   ____.

3. 그는 16층에 산다. (lives / floor / on the sixteenth / He)

   ____.

4. 7마리의 새가 하늘을 난다. (Seven / in the sky / birds / fly)

   ____.

5. 11월은 열한 번째 달이다. (is / month / the eleventh / November)

   ____.

A 영어는 우리말로, 우리말은 영어로 쓰세요.

❶ thousand	________	⓫ 사람들	________
❷ dollar	________	⓬ 해, 연	________
❸ cent	________	⓭ 12월	________
❹ May	________	⓮ 크리스마스	________
❺ April	________	⓯ 인형	________
❻ March	________	⓰ 100, 백	________
❼ zero	________	⓱ 오늘	________
❽ shoes	________	⓲ 2월	________
❾ number	________	⓳ 9월	________
❿ gloves	________	⓴ 장난감 자동차	________

B 괄호 안에서 알맞은 것을 고르세요.

❶ Children's Day is on (May fifth / May fiveth).

❷ Tomorrow is (July the four / July the fourth).

❸ This is the year (nineteen ninety / nineteen ninetieth).

❹ This book is two dollars (sixtieth / sixty) cents.

❺ They travel for five hundred (forty / fortieth) days.

❻ The day after tomorrow is (September fourth / September the four).

❼ This pen is four dollars (eighty / eightieth) cents.

❽ Her birthday is November (first / oneth).

❾ Two (thousands / thousand) seven is the Year of the Pig.

❿ There are one thousand two (hundred / hundredth) students.

C 괄호 안에 주어진 단어를 이용해서 빈칸을 완성하세요.

1. Children's Day is on ________________. (May / fifth)
2. Tomorrow is ________________. (the fourth / July)
3. This is ________________. (nineteen / ninety)
4. This book is ________________. (two dollars / sixty cents)
5. They travel for ________________. (five hundred / forty days)
6. The day after tomorrow is ________________. (fourth / September)
7. This pen is ________________. (eighty cents / four dollars)
8. Her birthday is ________________. (November / first)
9. ________________ is the Year of the Pig. (Two thousand / seven)
10. There are ________________ students. (two hundred / one thousand)

D 우리말과 같도록 괄호 안의 말을 이용해서 문장을 완성하세요.

1. 어린이날은 5월 5일이다. (Children's Day / fifth / on May / is)

   ____ .

2. 올해는 1990년이다. (ninety / nineteen / the year / This / is)

   ____ .

3. 이 펜은 4달러 80센트다. (This pen / eighty cents / four dollars / is)

   ____ .

4. 1,200명의 학생들이 있다. (There / two hundred / students / one thousand / are)

   ____ .

5. 그들은 540일 동안 여행한다. (They / forty days / five hundred / travel for)

   ____ .

Memo

Memo

완전 정복 초등 영문법

기출문제 3회

3

A*List

완전 정복 초등 영문법

기출문제 4회

3

A*List